Specially printed by the makers of Chicken Soup
for the Pet Lover's Soul™ brand dog and cat food.

Remember to always give the best to your pet.

CHICKEN SOUP
FOR THE SOUL®
CELEBRATES DOGS

and the People Who Love Them

A Collection in Words and Photographs by
Jack Canfield & Mark Victor Hansen
and
Sharon J. Wohlmuth

Health Communications, Inc.
Deerfield Beach, Florida

www.hcibooks.com
www.chickensoup.com

Subject matter, locality and/or people in the photographs may not be the actual locality or people in the stories. Names of certain individuals have been changed to protect their identity.

Library of Congress Cataloging-in-Publication Data

Chicken soup for the soul celebrates dogs and the people who love them : a collection in words and photographs / [edited by] by Jack Canfield & Mark Victor Hansen and Sharon J. Wohlmuth.

    p. cm.
  ISBN 0-7573-0147-9

  1. Dogs—United States—Anecdotes. 2. Dog owners—United States—Anecdotes.
3. Human-animal relationships—United States—Anecdotes. I. Canfield, Jack, 1944–
II. Hansen, Mark Victor. III. Wohlmuth, Sharon J.

SF426.2.C456 2004
636.7—dc22

2004054808

Publisher: Health Communications, Inc.
          3201 S.W. 15th Street
          Deerfield Beach, FL 33442-8190

Cover design by Larissa Hise Henoch
Inside book design by Dawn Von Strolley Grove

CONTENTS

Swimming the Mianus   *Carlo DeVito* 3

Carry on, Mister Boy   *Marky Olson* 16

Rita and Andy   *Lewis D. Lazorwitz*..24

Lonely Soul   *Sherwin Kaufman* 34

My First Babies   *Beth Josolowitz* 40

Mr. Utley's Gift   *Nicholas Hyde*...47

One Soul, Two Halves   *Ellen Urbani Hiltebrand*...54

Christmas with TwylaRose   *Emma Mellon* 63

Come Home, Sally, Come Home   *Dena Mosk Erwin* 73

The Comfort of a Cold, Wet Nose   *Barbara Baumgardner*.........................83

Contributors 88

Permissions 90

**ogs are not our whole life, but they make our lives whole.**

—Roger Caras

SWIMMING THE MIANUS

My parents used to have a beautiful white clapboard house on the banks of the Mianus River, in Connecticut. The smallish river lolled past beautiful houses, dotted with green lawns, gray docks, white Adirondack chairs and small colorful boats. My parents' house had a huge lawn that rolled down to the water. Looking across the water, you could see small boats at anchor, with their empty, rickety lobster pots stacked like building blocks thrown in a pile, bobbing up and down on the shining water. On the most memorable days, the sky was blue, the grass bright green and the whites blinding—a perfect postcard.

It was on such a day that Exley, my year-and-a-half-old German shorthaired pointer, decided he would go for a swim.

He was young and sturdy and precocious. He romped around, tough and strong, still with the youthful energy and excitement of a puppy.

Exley had a solid dark chocolate head, with three large liver patches, gray flecking and white socks. He was not exceptionally big, but he had a broad chest and alert eyes. He could be a terror one minute and an absolute sweetheart the next. A hunting machine, he liked nothing better than to fall asleep with his head on my lap. He was affectionate to a fault. But his penchant for chasing squirrels, birds, cats and other animals never ended well—especially for him.

Exley loved my parents' backyard, and was fond of rooting around in the shore's black, fine, oozy mud. Though my mother loved Exley, she was never very happy to see him arrive at her house, despite my protestations, for some mischief was always imminent. This particular day was no different.

Exley and I had been working on his training, and I decided here in the quiet of my parents' unfenced backyard would be a good time to reinforce my position as the alpha male in our limited pack of two.

"Siiiit," I said quietly, stepping back slowly. "Sit." I used an even, forceful tone. And it was working. I was now about twenty-five paces away. I stopped and commanded evenly again, "Down, Exley. Down." He got down and stayed down, and I began moving a little farther, and a little farther back. I was the master, I was the alpha male, I was in control. Finally, I was fifty to sixty paces away on our second attempt at the exercise, when I said, "Good boy, Exley! Good boy." I said this at the end, because no matter how I said it, quietly, excitedly, evenly, Exley would break. He was consistent in this. No matter the tone, he always broke when I praised him.

Now, Exley had always been good at coming back to me. And here he was, running toward me. Ears flapping up and down, his big pink tongue flopping like a rag doll from his mouth, a puppyish prance in his step, he bounced toward me. Suddenly, his eyes narrowed, his ears pricked up, his tongue drew in and his mouth closed. His gait changed from a bouncy trot to a thundering gallop. His powerful chest tightened, his stride exploded, and he raced down the slope of my parents' lawn like a horse in the Light Brigade. I tried to step in his way, but he barely lost stride, changing directions with speed and accuracy not seen since the Roman cavalry. I did not exist.

The ground shook as he approached and then shot past me. Though I felt some trepidation, and even as I was hollering, "Exley, come here!" at the top of my lungs, I could not help but admire his grace and elegance while in a full burst of pure speed. His body bobbed like an engine piston, with the grace of a thoroughbred, but his head stayed fixed like a cheetah in mid-hunt.

And then he leapt. I can still remember yelling "Nooooo," in slow motion, like in a bad Burt Reynolds movie. His leap was magnificent. In mid-air, he was the image of artful grace. He rose high over the shimmering water, his front paws elegantly stretched out before him, his hind legs balancing his back, and his Goofy-like ears flapping up in the wind. And into the beautiful New England postcard Exley leapt. His splash broke the silence that only existed in the motion picture inside my head.

"Exley, come! Exley, come here now! *Exley!*" But there was no penetrating his thick head. I scanned the water. There were three boats in the vicinity. But where was he going? There were no birds. He had been known to swim after ducks and seagulls. He was obsessed with game of any kind. I called and called but he did not heed me. He paddled furiously. One boat missed him. Another boat passed and obscured my view. None of these distracted him. Then it occurred to me. He was swimming to the opposite shore!

"No! No! Come back!" I screamed and hollered, but Exley kept moving. Trying to peer between the boats and houses and other obstacles, I squinted to see what was drawing his attention. But I couldn't see a thing. I realized I needed to move quickly. I raced up the lawn, ran into the house, swiped the keys and raced to the car. I had to get to the other side.

I roared down the sun-dappled, crooked country road like Gene Hackman in *The French Connection*, honking at all those in my way. Getting there was no easy feat. I had to race up toward Route One, drive across the river and find the road on the opposite bank. It should have been easy, but Murphy's Law was like gravity at ten-plus that day. Finally, I raced down the road, finding the landmarks I had picked out before I left.

I searched the riverbank. I looked at houses he might have been tempted to investigate. I checked out a couple of garbage bins where he might have been tempted to dine. I worried he might have been killed by an oncoming car. I drove up and down the street making sure he wasn't crumpled on the side of the road. *What had I done?! Oh, how could I let something happen to him?* It was then that I noticed that on the opposite shore, people on a passing boat were pointing to something. It was Exley, crawling back onto land . . . onto my parents' lawn. He was emerging from the tidal waters, covered in mud, rising like some canine version of the *Creature from the Black Lagoon*. He shook himself off, his large ears flapping and his stubby little tail wagging away. I was never so happy in my life. He was safe!

Just as suddenly as he had bolted passed me into the water, I now saw him bolting toward my parents' house. The patio door was open, and again it seemed I had entered some bad made-for-television movie. He bounded faster and faster, coated in earthy slime, up the trimly cut lawn, toward the striped-awning covered patio and my parents' house. "Noooooooo!"

Exley was banished from my parents' house that day. The mud had been tracked through the entire house. My mother screamed at him. My father screamed at him. I screamed at him. I yanked him outside to give him a bath, and when I was sure my parents weren't anywhere near, I got on the ground, and hugged him as never before. And I laughed; I laughed so heartily. I laughed because I loved him and was so happy he was alive. He licked my face and wagged his stubby little tail. He smelled awful, simply awful, and I hugged him all the more.

Carlo DeVito

The great pleasure of a dog is that you may make a fool of yourself with him and not only will he not scold you, he will make a fool of himself too.

—Samuel Butler

on't accept your dog's admiration as conclusive evidence that you are wonderful.

—Ann Landers

His name was Jasper, but to us, he was Mister Boy.

Eight weeks after he was born, we picked up our golden retriever puppy at the Seattle Airport following his flight from the Canine Companions for Independence Training Center in Santa Rosa, California. My husband and I, along with our two teenage daughters, had volunteered to be puppy raisers because we thought it would be a meaningful experience. It was. Only our collective sense of humor got us through puppyhood with Jasper.

Since we already owned Chester, a neurotic cockapoo, and two cats, Jasper had a lot of adjusting to do. However, puppies do not adjust. The people and other pets around them do. The cats relegated him to the bottom of the pet hierarchy, but Jasper didn't catch on. He assumed a "good-boy-sit" would atone for any of his antics.

When I worked at the computer, Jasper would sit under my desk and I could be fairly certain he was not getting into trouble. The remaining hours of the day were another matter. When anyone in the family lost something, we learned to look outside. Jasper had a penchant for taking anything he could get into his mouth and carting it out through the pet door to the garden. Anything not permanently attached to the ground or house was stolen and carted out. I would go out every few days just to clean out the garden. One would think we didn't keep a close enough watch on him, but he had learned to work quickly. Then there were the items that wouldn't fit through the pet door. A yardstick, for instance, won't fit horizontally, but is easily chewed in half. One day, my daughter looked out the upstairs window and screamed, "Mom! Why is there laundry all over the garden?" An entire load of just-cleaned clothes was strewn across the lawn. Another time, I got the grocery bags only as far as the laundry room. A short time later Jasper trotted into the kitchen covered in white powder and did a "good-boy-sit." Panic set in. It was a long time before I could laugh about the mess a puppy can make with a ten-pound bag of flour.

But eighteen months later, as we said good-bye to him at the airport, we wondered what we had been thinking. We simply wanted to keep him. I thought my heart would break.

A year later this memory was balanced with the joy of seeing Jasper graduate in CCI's social dog program. I looked deeply into his brown eyes—I wanted him to know how much we missed him. He knew.

Jasper had been assigned to Stacie, an occupational therapist who would take him to work with her every day at a Salem,

Oregon hospital. I shared lunch with Stacie and all of the other new owners, their new canine graduates and the CCI folks who had made it all possible. No one entering the banquet room would have known there were twelve dogs in faithful "down-stays" under their respective new owners' tables. The new owners had been in Santa Rosa for two weeks of intensive training with their dogs.

The moving ceremony told the powerful story of the human-animal connection. There was Yenti, the service dog who had been assigned to a fourteen-year-old nonverbal autistic boy. Within a short time, this boy had begun to verbalize his love for "my Yenti." Unger, another canine-in-training, had been on an outing to a local shopping center with a CCI trainer. A man near them had suddenly passed out. During the next half hour of action with paramedics, Unger never left the man's side, knowing only that this stranger was in peril and needed his support. The ceremony ended with a woman in a wheelchair singing "You Light Up My Life." Her dog, sharing the spotlight with her, sat patiently, eyes never leaving her new owner's face.

Two years later, my daughter and I were able to visit Stacie and Jasper at work in Salem and by then I was able to view our time with Jasper as one link in the chain of caring. His brown eyes still tugged at me, but so too did the sparkle in a patient's eye as he laboriously reached from his bed to stroke Jasper's fur.

Several years had passed when a card arrived from Stacie. Jasper had been diagnosed with cancer and his front leg had been amputated. His brown eyes again flooded my memory as I told my husband and our now-grown daughters. But this is when I learned who our Mister Boy really was. It seemed that Jasper did not realize he was disabled. He not only returned to work, but he was able to accomplish everything he had done before, even learning to "shake paws" by balancing on his hind legs. His inspiration became hauntingly apparent to Stacie's patients when many of them said, "If Jasper can do it, so can I!"

Now I understand Jasper's legacy—if only we could all just learn to use our grief and pain as fuel for our journeys. He continued his work until November 2001. Then we heard from Stacie that the cancer had returned. Jasper is gone now, but never his spirit. Carry on, Mister Boy.

Marky Olson

e give dogs time we can spare, space we can spare and love we can spare. And in return, dogs give us their all. It's the best deal man has ever made.

—Margery Facklam

RITA AND ANDY

It is a quiet, still evening. Rita sits on the wide window ledge looking out on the street below, allowing her thoughts to drift, much like the soft clouds overhead. But she quickly returns her attention to the street below. She turns her head back and forth, looking at the passing throngs of people as they make their way home from work. Some she recognizes as they wave to her, others are strangers who do nothing more than give her a passing glance or a smile.

At middle age, Rita is still graceful and elegant with a youthful exuberance. Her brown eyes sparkle with joy. Her hair is luxurious and has a glossy sheen. Her walk is more of a strut and she holds her head high knowing she often gets a second glance. Her legs are straight, muscular and strong. Truth be told though, Rita could care less about her youthful appearance and the appreciative glances she receives.

Her life is filled with happiness and love, all for one man. He is the reason she waits at the window every night, just so she can get that first glimpse of him as he emerges from the crowd. She knows that after that first glimpse she'll have enough time to prepare herself for his arrival home; but until then she keeps her vigil at the window.

When Andy and Rita first met they knew in an instant their relationship was meant for life. After their first night together their bond was unbreakable. They became inseparable and knew that they had been destined for each other. A match that happens only once in a lifetime, they were devoted one to the other, sharing a deep love, till death do them part.

Finally Rita spots Andy in the crowd. It would be hard to miss his bouncing stride and his head bobbing from side to side like some bouncing ball on top of a "sing-a-long" tune on TV. She feels the excitement rising in her as it always has. After all their time together, you would think this childish exuberance would have passed, but Rita still has those butterflies, same as she did the first time they came back to the apartment together.

She moves away from the window, taking a quick survey of the apartment, then stops in the middle of the room and waits. She hears Andy's keys in the lock and gazes at him as he steps into the apartment. As soon as Andy empties his arms into the nearest chair, Rita rushes to greet him. Now that he's home, the apartment is safe and warm. They sit together on the couch and joyfully kid with each other.

After supper Andy slips into a pair of jeans and an L.A. Dodgers sweatshirt. As he emerges from the bedroom he turns to Rita and says, "How about going for a walk?" It's a rhetorical question,

Rita is already waiting as Andy puts on his coat.

They step from the apartment together and Andy closes the door behind them. There on the door is a brass plaque that reads "RITA" (rottweiler in the apartment). Andy puts Rita's leash on her and off they go, *man and his best friend*!

Lewis D. Lazorwitz

o matter what, a dog will love you unconditionally.

—Anonymous

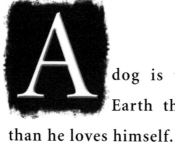dog is the only thing on Earth that loves you more than he loves himself.

—Josh Billings

He is your friend, your partner, your defender, your dog. You are his life, his love, his leader. He will be yours, faithful and true, to the last beat of his heart. You owe it to him to be worthy of such devotion.

—Unknown

LONELY SOUL

He can't remember Mom
Never knew his dad
A dog was his companion
The only friend he had

He had a brother somewhere
Who never kept in touch
There was no love between them
So he wasn't missing much

The world can be a lonely place
And folks can be unkind
We hunger for affection, but
True love is hard to find

He loved his childhood sweetheart
And thought she loved him too
Until the day she told him
She found somebody new

So he reached out to others
Till he was old and gray
But found no one to love him
And then he passed away

The world can be a lonely place
And folks can be unkind
We hunger for affection, but
True love is hard to find

They say that when you die
And reach the other side
The one who loves you most
Becomes your spirit guide

And when he did cross over
He saw to his surprise
A tail that wagged so happily
And faithful, loving eyes

Sherwin Kaufman

**A**cquiring a dog may be the only opportunity a human ever has to choose a relative.

—Mordecai Siegal

MY FIRST BABIES

When my son Philip was born, I already knew how to love and tend to a vulnerable, dependent being.

I had become a mommy at the tender age of fourteen. The fact that my offspring was a seven-week-old Irish setter puppy was irrelevant from my perspective. I felt maternal, protective and extremely proud. My affection for Misty Dawn (a name only a young adolescent girl could adore) planted the seed for a more mature motherly love. This maternal seed bloomed when I was twenty-eight years old and the new mother of a seven-pound baby boy.

I learned a lot from raising a puppy as a young girl. Being the youngest of three children I did not have little siblings to care for, nor upon whom to practice my innate mothering skills. Misty was the first living creature for whom I was responsible. When she chewed my clothing, shredded my underwear or destroyed my contact lens case, I came to understand the need for patience. When she cried and barked upon my return from school, I learned she needed to be walked and have some playtime. Misty had a beautiful, long, shiny auburn coat that I brushed until she practically sparkled. I developed a sense of pride regarding my ability to care for my dog.

Although it wasn't always comfortable or enjoyable, I learned to place another's needs above my own. This was essential for nurturing any living being, whether a furry beast or hairless baby. Being awakened at 3 A.M. whether for the puppy's full bladder or my baby's empty stomach, I would groggily sleepwalk down the hall. Puppy shots and baby shots, little puddles of pee on the kitchen floor or next to the toilet, were part and parcel of being Mommy to dog or baby. The need for attention and comfort, whether playing doggie tug-of-war with Misty or building towers with Philip's blocks, offering Milk-Bones to my pup or vanilla wafers to my toddler, all seemed related.

I have a picture of Philip and Misty cuddling together that always brings me a bittersweet feeling when I gaze at it. It was taken the day of Philip's bris, an important ceremony in the Jewish faith that seals the child's covenant with God. Many family members were present at the ceremony and I mourned for those who were not. I was also deeply joyful as I looked at my son, feeling immeasurably blessed and thrilled beyond words at becoming a mother to this beautiful baby. It was at this moment that I realized just how much Misty had contributed to my life. She had taught me to love and care, to hold my anger, to overlook the messes: the poopies, the chewed-up books and records. She had helped to teach me that inconvenience was just that—

inconvenience and nothing more. She had taught me that in the grand scheme of things it is the love, the laughs, the incredibly long walks a dog of her nature demands that count, and that even tears bring richness and meaning to life.

My time with her was coming to an end and life with my son was just beginning. I looked over to Misty, now old and graying but still gentle and affectionate. My beautiful first babies, one canine, one human. Both loved.

Beth Josolowitz

Whoever said you can't buy happiness forgot about puppies.

—Gene Hill

MR. UTLEY'S GIFT

Mr. Utley is a big, loving hound mix that lives up the street on the cul-de-sac. He has been our Jessica's best friend since Scott and Mary Fuller brought him to our neighborhood. Jessica, by the way, is our Lab-golden mix full of limitless bounding energy and love of life. One of her favorite things in the whole world is the two or three times a week when Mr. Utley comes to play at our house.

Mr. Utley is an accomplished escape artist. Despite Scott and Mary's best efforts, he manages to find his way through any available opening to his friend Jessica's house for a round of doggy play. We usually invite him into the yard if we're home and let the dogs have their fun. Then, either Scott or Mary will come looking for him (they always know where to look) or one of us will escort him home on a leash.

When Jessica developed a terrible case of kennel cough, besides sounding terrible with the racking dry hack, she had to be isolated from all her doggy friends until the antibiotics killed off every last infectious bug. We called all our dog-owner friends including Scott and Mary and gave them the bad news. Jessica could have no company for at least a week—an eternity for our very social pup and longer than she had ever gone without her friend Mr. Utley.

Of course, the inevitable happened a few days later. We saw Mr. Utley arrive outside our fence looking for his best friend. I had to restrain Jessica so she couldn't contact Mr. Utley and risk infecting him. My wife, Penny, grabbed the extra leash and led him back around the corner to home. When Mr. Utley was safely away, I let Jessica go so she could run over and investigate where her friend had been. She bolted across the yard and reached outside the fence to grab something in her mouth. When I caught up with her I found her munching on a very large dog biscuit that had been left just within her reach. I thought that maybe Penny had carried it outside to entice Mr. Utley to come along with her so she could get the leash on him. I didn't see much sense in that, though, because Mr. Utley was such a friendly dog, he would generally come running up to anyone remotely interested in him.

"Did you try to give Mr. Utley a biscuit when you went to get him?" I asked Penny when she returned.

"No, I didn't," she replied.

"Well then, who left the biscuit outside the fence where Mr. Utley was standing?"

It only took a second to solve the mystery. Mr. Utley had missed his friend so much that he wanted to bring her a "get well soon" gift. As a token of his devotion to his friend, he carried his own dog biscuit down from his house to give to his best friend, Jessica.

Nicholas Hyde

door is what a dog is perpetually on the wrong side of.

—Ogden Nash

ONE SOUL, TWO HALVES

My husband remarks in reference to Cali and me, "I have never known an animal and a human who were more like two halves of the same soul."

I was a young teacher working in a foreign country and Cali a two-month-old ball of matted fur when we first met. I had thought that a German shepherd would be a good companion for a single female living alone in a remote village. Big and robust by four-and-a-half months, Cali stepped on a scorpion that was ambling across the porch one night. Cali was quickly reduced to an immobile, lethargic pup. How she managed to live through the incident I do not know; a friend's puppy, two weeks younger, had died from such a bite within two hours.

Cali lived, but she was completely paralyzed. She could not even move her mouth to eat, so I fed her by dripping raw egg down the back of her throat. She developed a blood infection and high fever from the wound, so I carried her across the country on rattletrap buses to an American vet, who put her on IV fluids for a week and then sent us home, saying there was nothing more to be done. Nonetheless, I collected water at night and submerged her in it during the day to control her fever. So we lived like this for over a month: I, at five feet three and one hundred pounds, carrying a forty-pound, paralyzed dog across my shoulders everywhere I went, and she defying death.

Having spent so much time carrying her around with me to monitor her health, I felt it was silly to leave her home once she recovered and was able to get around on her own. She hiked with me through the mountains and curled up under a child's desk each day in the rural schools where I taught. She ate her dinner next to me on the dirt floor each night. We were constant companions and best friends, and to this day I can think of nothing we would not do for each other.

Not that I needed proof of this loyalty, but she demonstrated it one night after I'd moved to a house with a bedroom that opened directly onto an enclosed courtyard. The outer double doors were made of two pieces of wood, which were attached to the adobe walls with rusty nails and supported inside by a two-by-four. A strong wind could have knocked them down. Cali's growls woke me in the middle of the night as she stood guard over me on top of the bed, facing the door with her teeth bared. I heard footsteps on the concrete patio outside, advancing slowly toward the bedroom door. Never in my twenty-four years had the implications of a sound been clearer to me; never had I been more terrified. While I had rehearsed such a scenario in my head countless times—how I would defend myself with quick kicks to the shin and groin and blows to the bridge of the nose—when the moment to act presented itself, I was immobilized by fear. I could not even move my arm to reach for the knife I kept hidden under my pillow. I lay there, unable to breathe, sure I would suffocate before the man outside had a chance to kill me. The footsteps echoed closer, and still I could not move.

As the intruder threw his body against the door to break through, Cali leapt from the bed, and their bodies hit the two wooden boards at exactly the same time. Through the cracks in the wood, she clawed at him with her paws and slashed at him with her teeth. Still he persisted. Every time he stepped back and flung his body at the door to break it down from the outside, she flung her body at it from the inside and held up that rickety old door. After what seemed like an eternity, he ran off—as scared of my dog as I had been of him. This time it was she who saved me.

The more time we spent together, the closer we became, until the similarities between us seemed almost eerie. Whenever I got a cold, so did Cali. When my allergies got bad after we'd returned to the States, Cali developed allergies too, and after a series of tests, it was determined that we were actually allergic to the same foods and pollens. When my allergies improved, so did hers. At my wedding, a large outdoor affair, a friend held Cali on a leash throughout the ceremony. Just as the minister asked, "Do you take this man?" before I responded, "I do," a long, loud howl echoed from the back of the crowd. It was Cali, most surely saying, "I do too."

Unfortunately, the similarities did not end there. Six months after I was diagnosed with a benign heart murmur, Cali was also diagnosed with a heart murmur. We were driving cross-country on our honeymoon with Cali in the backseat. She had developed a weepy eye, and I was concerned some road dust was irritating it, so we stopped at a veterinary hospital in Salt Lake City to have it checked. The vet looked at her eyes, then as part of the routine exam put the stethoscope to Cali's chest. His forehead furrowed and he bit his lip as he moved the stethoscope across her body for a full five minutes. Finally, he straightened up and addressed us. "Her eyes are fine," he said, "but she has a serious heart condition." As I held her and cried, the vet performed an ultrasound to confirm his diagnosis: subaortic stenosis. There really was nothing to be done; the cardiac specialist we took her to later said he had never heard a worse heart. "If you treat her normally, she has two months to live," he said. "But if you keep her inside at all times, prevent her from running around or exerting any energy, she may have a life span of up to two years."

"I can't do that," I said. "She plays outside every day; we run together all the time. She'd be absolutely miserable locked up inside."

"Then you'll kill her," the vet said.

"But she'll die happy," I retorted. "I know she'd prefer a short, happy life to a long, miserable one." Though devastated at her prognosis, I relished the opportunity to ensure that the end of her life would be fun and happy.

That was well over three years ago. Cali and I walk or jog a couple of miles to the park every day—depending on my own level of stamina—where she plays with a pack of dog friends and swims in the river. She has traveled back and forth across the country twice more, has hiked the redwood forest, and is so healthy that the only reason we go to the vet anymore is to update her vaccines. Oh, her heart is still in terrible condition. In fact, whenever we do go to the vet, the staff always asks politely if everyone in the office can listen to it. "You'll never hear a heart like this again," they say to one another. The vet admits he has never seen a healthier looking dog with a worse heart, and adds that there is no medical explanation for her longevity.

I can explain it, though. Cali teaches me every day that there are forces greater than medicine and technology. From the minute she recovered from that scorpion bite, she has repaid my nurturing with unwavering loyalty and friendship. She has been the guardian not only of my physical body but also of my soul. In times of loneliness and fear, she has again and again offered herself wholeheartedly and unselfishly to me. Out of love for me, she continues to live.

I am no fool; I know that eventually Cali will die. Nonetheless, I have had the opportunity to share my soul with a wise and generous teacher. When I needed it most, God sent me an angel disguised in fur to remind me of the power of love.

Ellen Urbani Hiltebrand

CHRISTMAS WITH TWYLAROSE

When I adopted TwylaRose, a retired racing greyhound, I promised myself I would treat her like a dog and not like a four-legged imitation human. She was my first dog and I had my standards. There'd be no dressing up in human clothes, no Christmas photographs with Santa, no joint shopping trips, no jewelry and no baby talk. I resolved to preserve her dog-ness and my dignity.

Those high sentiments crashed, one by one, beginning with the restrictions against baby talk. Though I didn't actually make goo-goo sounds on the way home from the kennel, I brimmed over with pet names: Pumpkin, Sweetie, Girlfriend, Honeybunch, Boo. . . . I hadn't expected to feel so much or to feel it so quickly.

The skinny anxious creature in the backseat spoke directly to my heart. Our first hour together transformed me into her friend and protector, parent and pal, teacher and student, sister and most dedicated fan.

As our first Halloween approached, a friend bought a top hat and tails costume for her own dog. Theoretically, I couldn't have been more opposed to the idea but it got me thinking. I enjoy Halloween and it didn't seem right to leave TwylaRose out of the festivities.

Since she came from the long line of hounds that lived as royalty with the pharaohs, I dressed her as Anubis, the deity in Egyptian mythology whose task it was to lead the deceased into the other world. Anubis appears in tomb paintings as a half-human, half-greyhound figure that weighs the human heart against its own truth in the form of a feather.

Being helped through that final passage by a god with the

canine qualities of faithfulness and surefooted instinct appealed to me. I assured myself that TwylaRose as Anubis was not only a species-appropriate character, but one that was inspirational and educational as well.

I sewed a golden-brown sequined body suit and a small matching bag to hold the feather. Of course no one had a clue about who she was supposed to be. Even when I explained, no one much cared and TwylaRose seemed indifferent, but I enjoyed recounting the mythology and I loved the flash of sunlight off those sequins.

During that first year, I had become friends with three women who also had adopted retired racers. Our four greys became The Pack: TwylaRose, Ike, Pepper and Christa. With humans in tow, they met several times a week.

Nothing pleased the greyhounds so much as being together. They sniffed butts, stood flank to flank in greeting and draped their long necks over each other. When it was too hot or too cold to walk, we met at someone's home where the greys vied for squeaky toys or came to us for stroking, then settled into naps. Doggy play dates became part of my reality and an extended human/canine family formed.

When Christmas approached, somebody suggested we have The Pack's picture taken with Santa Claus. My early resolutions echoed against the idea but I felt the tug: Wouldn't it be sweet? Wouldn't it be fun? Wouldn't it be nice to have a picture of The Pack?

I cast around for an excuse to break my own rule. *Since I am no fan of Christmas excesses,* I reasoned, *the photo could be my Wegman-like comment on the season. Everyone else wants to go and it would be rude of me to resist.* I said I'd do it for the good of the group. Of course, I lied. Deep down, I wanted to immortalize our Pack. I wanted to include them in our celebration of winter, like the family members they were. So I went along. I even tied a wide red ribbon around TwylaRose's neck and stiffened it with a shot of spray starch.

And so we found ourselves at PetSmart one Saturday morning just before Christmas. A large pet supply chain store, PetSmart welcomes dogs to shop along with their humans. It hosts events like meet-and-greets during which various rescue groups show their dogs and take applications for adoption. In December, they host Santa.

The store was rich with the scents of dogs as well as the subtle perfume of live snakes, kittens, iguana, parakeets and parrots. It was a huge cavernous place with fluorescent light pouring down on a crowd of shoppers and their sniffing animal companions, frantic from overstimulation. Exotic birds, parrots and canaries layered the air with their cries and Burl Ives tied it all up in a fat red ribbon with his hearty and optimistic rendition of "Jingle Bell Rock."

Just inside the door, Ike began trembling so hard his tags rattled. Pepper and TwylaRose lunged in opposite directions, and Christa hid her tail and froze. We had arrived early to avoid the crowd. Santa's white plastic bench waited at the center of the store. We stood second in line. Christa eyed the chihuahua ahead of us, her predator instinct stirring. Pepper's anxiety turned to gas, heralding intestinal distress. By now, Ike was vibrating and TwylaRose had lowered her head and was pulling toward the door.

Santa slunk in from a back room. He was human, small and shapeless. He didn't look like the Santa in the Macy's Thanksgiving Day Parade. His shoulders rounded and his face hung expressionless until it disappeared into a tired, synthetic beard.

I felt empathy for Santa. I wouldn't want to spend my Saturday posing with overwrought dogs and trying to please their doting owners. Our Santa coped by exhibiting an indifference of mythic proportions. He sat down. The feisty chihuahua sprinted toward him and spun at his feet. Santa stared straight ahead. The human scooped up her darling and plopped him onto Santa's lap. She crouched just outside of camera range and cheered her pup on. The Polaroid flashed and it was our turn.

Trembling, farting, panting, scanning the environment for danger, tongues hanging out, ears up to monitor sounds, the greys approached for the group picture.

Santa sat there limp while we arranged the greyhounds around him, TwylaRose beside him on the bench and Christa up on the other side. TwylaRose jumped down and I lifted her up again. We draped Santa's arms over each of the girls and wrapped the fingers of his gloved hands around their collars. We arranged Ike to the right of his knees and Pepper to the left. We backed out of camera sight, holding our collective breath. Pepper broke for the door. We set him back into place.

One camera flash and it was done. We each have a copy. There is Pepper looking for the exit, Ike with his long, long tongue panting into the camera, TwylaRose whose red bow had slipped down her neck and Christa smiling at the lens.

I still believe TwylaRose deserves respect for who she is. There are still no dog pajamas in the house, though on cold nights I do throw a light blanket over her. I shop alone at the pet store. The baby talk comes and goes and mixes with adult conversations. Every Christmas I bring out the picture of The Pack with Santa. I'm learning about what it is to be a greyhound, racing and retired. And she participates when I involve us in human adventures. I may have trashed my standards but I've come to understand that tasting each other's lives is the point, and love, not foolishness, enables that to happen.

Emma Mellon

COME HOME, SALLY, COME HOME

She sleeps peacefully in the big, old leather armchair. It is winter and the air outside is cold. Her long, golden coat is silken and clean. She is warm, quiet and comfortable. With gentle rubs and tender pats, she has drifted off to wherever it is that dogs go to dream. When she wakes she will nuzzle my hand, asking for more. Her eyes will sparkle and her face will shine with the warmth of a thousand sunbeams. My heart will feel each one as if Cupid's arrows were in charge of them all. Yes, I am in love with Sally. And she is finally in love with me.

Throughout her younger years, long before we even moved to the farm, Sally lived up the road from our place. A frightened and injured young pup, she had wandered into our neighbor's yard some ten years earlier and became a one-man dog, loyal forever to her master who patiently required nothing of her and gave her all that he could. When her master became widowed and old, it became necessary for him to move to town to live with his daughter. Sally, who lived in the garage, had to stay behind—alone. She was steadfast in her devotion to her master who visited several times each week, bringing her a supply of food and welcome companionship. Passersby along the rural road would see Sally sitting faithfully, waiting at the driveway's edge. Seasons would come and go; yet Sally stayed. We tried to make friends with her; after all, we were neighbors, but she would have nothing of it and each time we approached her she would scurry off as if we were alien beings full of some repugnant scent.

The march of time played on and another winter arrived with a vengeance, this one colder and more punishing than the one before. Sally's elderly master became ill and required hospitalization and surgery. He could not come to care for her. Still, she waited faithfully, seeking his face among the family members who came in his place. She longed for her master, her friend, and for the comfort of his touch, the warmth of his voice. Surely, she could not know why he did not come. Or could she?

We took over the activity of feeding her and twice daily walked or drove through the snow and cold temperatures to deliver food, fresh water and friendship. We knew we were making progress when Sally actively greeted us, coming out from behind her boarded shelter in the drafty, old, open garage. We were gratified by this development, but for a long while she still would not let us near enough to touch her. The bitter cold and deep snowdrifts kept her aging frame shivering and our concern for her grew. We offered her a straw-filled doghouse that she humbly declined, preferring instead the makeshift shelter her master had prepared for her.

On the morning of her master's surgery at the actual time the surgery was underway, my husband was at the house putting Sally's food out. When he left, she followed him back down the snowy road to our house! He called me out to witness this incredible moment. While Sally poised carefully, I knelt down and reached out to gather her face in my arms. She sat perfectly still, as though in complete surrender. Our eyes met in a moment of such clarity that I knew we had shared a glimpse of each other's soul. Then she turned and went up the road without looking back. While feeding her several days later, I told Sally that I didn't think her master was going to be able to come back anymore. I told her it would be a good idea if she just came to live with us. "Come home," I told her, "Sally, come home."

A day or so afterward, my husband drove up the road to feed her. With his hands full of food, he climbed out of the truck and walked through the heavy snow toward the garage. The truck door remained open. Sally eagerly came out to greet him, trotted right past him and leaped into the truck for the ride *home*! Could she have possibly understood what I had related to her earlier? In my heart I believe so.

Once integrated into her new family of ten other dogs and seven cats, Sally found new verve and expression, both vocal and physical. She relaxed, gained weight and joyfully interacted with us all, even our visitors! She spends most of her time indoors now, relishing the comfort and enjoying the attention. In the evenings when the outside dogs are snug in their pens inside the barn, she will come and sit beside my chair. She keeps her eyes riveted on me, and I know she is asking to go outside where she will wander and explore in her solitary fashion until she is ready to come back in. Then, she comes to the patio door and waits patiently to be noticed and brought indoors. These new rituals are all so familiar now.

Occasionally, her old master's family brings him for a visit. Sally greets him unreservedly. There is a total look of adoration on her face and for an instant they connect completely, bridging all the missing moments that time and circumstances have robbed them of. They delight in each other's company for a while, knowing that their love for each other transcends time and space. They part peacefully. Her master leaves, Sally stays, never to be alone again.

Dena Mosk Erwin

y goal in life is to be as good a person as my dog already thinks I am.

—Unknown

THE COMFORT OF A COLD, WET NOSE

I hadn't even wanted a dog in the first place, but my husband had been insisting for months, so I finally relented. Soon Shawn was *my* dog, a friend and faithful companion. He didn't ask for any more than I was willing to give—a daily meal, a kind word, a warm bed—but not my bed. No dogs allowed on my bed!

A few years later, my husband died. My first night alone, I laid in bed staring into the darkness, my pillow wet with an unending flow of tears. The bed suddenly seemed so big all by myself. I wondered how long it would take for the loneliness to heal when I first felt it move. It was cold and clammy and creeping slowly into my open hand, outside the covers. The solid, cold, wet mass was followed by prickly hairs and just before I screamed, a muffled but familiar whine came from the creature who was forcing his cold, wet nose into my trembling hand.

"Oh, Shawn! What are you doing on my bed?" I threw my arms around his thick hairy neck and hugged him through my tears.

In the days and months that followed, I came to realize that this dog I hadn't wanted was truly a gift of love from God. He was a warm-fuzzy on my bed every night; a companion who was always willing and happy, available to go for a walk when I needed to get out of the house. Twice, he snapped at me as I was wailing loudly and out of control, as if to remind me to be strong and of good courage.

In the months that followed my husband's death, Shawn taught me about acceptance and forgiveness. The crazy dog loves me just as I am. From him I've learned to be a warm-fuzzy to those around me who are hurting and to approach them gently, loving them just as they are. Like my dog curled up by the warm fire, I just want to be there in case I'm needed. I thank God for providing a friend when I felt alone, and for the comfort of a cold, wet nose.

Barbara Baumgardner

Dogs are our link to paradise. They don't know evil or jealousy or discontent. To sit with a dog on a hillside on a glorious afternoon is to be back in Eden, where doing nothing was not boring—it was peace.

—Milan Kundera

CONTRIBUTORS

Barbara Baumgardner nests in Bend, Oregon, when not traveling in her motor home. She is a columnist for *RV Companion Magazine,* and a hospice volunteer, which inspired her first book, *A Passage Through Grief* and then *A Passage Through Divorce.*

Carlo DeVito has written several books including *The Everything Dog Book* and *The Everything Puppy Book.* His new book about his life with Exley is titled *10 Secrets My Dog Taught Me,* due out from Rodale in fall of 2005. Carlo is a publishing executive who lives in Freehold, New Jersey, with his wife, Dominique, his sons Dawson and Dylan, two dogs, and ten fancy goldfish.

Dena Mosk Erwin is a retired human resources director who lives with her husband on their sixty-acre White Oaks Farm, a true country place, in southern Illinois. They care for numerous rescued animals and horses and introduce young people to the wonderful world of animals. E-mail her at *dena@wabash.net.*

Ellen Hiltebrand was a Peace Corps volunteer in Guatemala from 1991 to 1993. Her dog, Cali, returned with her to the U.S. and lived a full life until she died in Ellen's arms in 1999. Publication is pending on a novel about the years they lived in Central America. Contact Ellen at *ellen@jen-elle.com.*

Nicholas Hyde lives, works and plays in San Diego, California, with his wife of twenty-seven years, Penny, and his four-year-old golden-Lab mix, Jessica. They all love long walks together, throwing tennis balls with their ChuckIt, and having dog friends over to romp in the backyard.

Beth Josolowitz is an animal lover, gardener and amateur knitter who grew up in Bristol, Connecticut, and now lives in Columbus, Ohio, with her two wonderful sons, Philip and Seth. They share their home with a rescued collie, two cats, a parrot and a little green turtle.

Sherwin Kaufman is a grandson of the legendary humorist, Shalom Aleichem, on whose stories *Fiddler on the Roof* is based. He is a retired physician with a new career as an award-winning composer, lyricist and poet. He can be reached at 212-744-5788.

Lewis Lazorwitz is a Vietnam veteran, a military retiree and a retired correctional sergeant of the California Department of Corrections. Lewis finds writing short stories a great way to relax. He will be returning to college to complete his degree in criminology.

Emma Mellon, Ph.D., is a writer and psychologist in private practice near Philadelphia who rarely works without at least one greyhound present. She is completing a memoir about her time with TwylaRose. Dr. Mellon's work has been published in the U.S. and Great Britain. E-mail her at *greygirltr@earthlink.net.*

Marky J. Olson lives in Sammamish, Washington, with her husband, golden retriever and two cats. She was a successful copywriter, model and is currently a high school English teacher. She is an avid reader, gardener and seamstress. She and her husband enjoy spending time with their grown children and taking advantage of all the northwest has to offer.

PERMISSIONS

Swimming the Mianus. Reprinted by permission of Carlo DeVito. ©2004 Carlo DeVito.

Carry on, Mister Boy. Reprinted by permission of Marky J. Olson. ©1998 Marky J. Olson.

Rita and Andy. Reprinted by permission of Lewis Lazorwitz. ©1996 Lewis Lazorwitz.

Lonely Soul. Reprinted by permission of Sherwin Kaufman. ©2003 Sherwin Kaufman.

My First Babies. Reprinted by permission of Beth Susan Josolowitz. ©2004 Beth Susan Josolowitz.

Mr. Utley's Gift. Reprinted by permission of Nicholas Hyde. ©2003 Nicholas Hyde.

One Soul, Two Halves. Reprinted by permission of Ellen Hiltebrand. ©1995 Ellen Hiltebrand.

Christmas with TwylaRose. Reprinted by permission of Emma Mellon. ©2004 Emma Mellon.

Come Home, Sally, Come Home. Reprinted by permission of Dena Mosk Erwin. ©2001 Dena Mosk Erwin.

The Comfort of a Cold, Wet Nose. Reprinted by permission of Barbara Jean Baumgardner. ©1985 Barbara Jean Baumgardner.